# Augustine of Hippo

by
Fr Ben O'Rourke OSA

*All booklets are published thanks to the
generous support of the members of the
Catholic Truth Society*

CATHOLIC TRUTH SOCIETY
PUBLISHERS TO THE HOLY SEE

2

## Contents

Early Years . . . . . . . . . . . . . . . . . . . . . . . . . . . . . . . . . . . . . . . . . .3

'I Hated School' . . . . . . . . . . . . . . . . . . . . . . . . . . . . . . . . . .8

In Love with Love . . . . . . . . . . . . . . . . . . . . . . . . . . . . . . .13

'An Unbelievable Fire in My Heart' . . . . . . . . . . . . . .16

'I Taught the Tricks of Speech' . . . . . . . . . . . . . . . . . .21

'Time to Put My Soul Together Again' . . . . . . . . . . . .24

Rome: 'The Wind Rose and Filled Our Sails' . . . . . . .27

'I Became More Unhappy, But You More Near' . . . . .34

'I Withdrew Completely Into Myself' . . . . . . . . . . . . .39

Time to be Still . . . . . . . . . . . . . . . . . . . . . . . . . . . . . . . . .48

'All Must be Loved' . . . . . . . . . . . . . . . . . . . . . . . . . . . .55

Prayers and Reflections by St Augustine . . . . . . . . . .65

Further reading . . . . . . . . . . . . . . . . . . . . . . . . . . . . . . . .66

# Early Years

When he was born, his parents gave him a name given to very few at the time. Custom would have preferred 'Patrick', his father's name. But, as his parents bent over the cradle of their newborn son, we can be sure that Monica, his mother, had a say in giving him the name 'Augustine'. It was so ambitious. They named him after the Emperor Augustus. So he was 'little Augustus', or 'little emperor'.

This boy, born to poor parents in a remote part of Rome's vast Empire, would make the name 'Augustine' even more famous than that of the illustrious emperor after whom he was called.

The year was 354, the place Thagaste, a little town, now called Souk Ahras on the border of present-day Algeria and Tunisia. The world in which he grew up was Roman Africa. It had been under Roman dominion for three centuries. The culture, the laws, the education were Roman, the language Latin. A century earlier this part of the Empire had been a place of economic boom, but by 354 the prosperity was fading.

His family were small property owners. Of his father's estate we know only of a small vineyard. Most of the people around lived from the land, working hard and paying heavy taxes. The family lived modestly, having to be frugal and avoid getting into debt.

It quickly became clear that the young boy was gifted, so his father saved and scraped to pay the taxes and to send his son to the best school available. His parents had high ambitions for him. They believed that a classical education was the way to help their bright young son to escape from the boredom and harshness of life in small-town Thagaste. The town had a wealthy patron, and as Augustine grew up he was able to see the lifestyle of this rich man. It was a lavish lifestyle, with an abundance of feasts, rich games, magnificent hunts, luxurious baths, and an impressive residence. It seemed to have dazzled the young boy and became a model which Augustine set before himself, if he were to escape the drudgery of his father's world.

So the family made sacrifices to send their son for three years to the grammar school at the nearby town of Madaurus. As we shall see, the strain of keeping him at the school told on the family, and his schooling was to be interrupted by lack of funds.

### 'The Confessions'

When Augustine comes to write the story of his life, he offers us not the record of happenings and events, but the story of his inner self. It is the story of his heart's journey. It is the story of his coming to discover and own his true self.

So there is much we do not know about his early years. What we do get from him is the story of his relationships, of his friendships, and of his troubled and anguished teenage struggles. Above all, we see how his inner life, at every step, was linked with his deep need of God, whom he resisted for half his seventy years.

He tells us little of the family's history. We don't even know for certain how many brothers and sisters he had. We know little of his father's status, or of his work. What we are given, instead, is one of the most fascinating accounts to be found anywhere in the world of a soul's struggles to be itself.

The influence of his parents on his inner development is of far more interest to him than their setting him on the road to a suitable career. His father had little influence on his growing up; his mother's was a very dominant influence. We are told of the tensions that came from his being the child of a mixed marriage, his father being a pagan and his mother a strong Catholic. Of his father Augustine says little. His silence seems to suggest a coldness in the relationship. He appreciated the hard work and the sacrifices his father had made to see him soundly educated. He admired his 'pigheaded resolution' to provide the best school. But their relationship was shallow. He relates how one day, at the public baths, his father had remarked on the signs of puberty in Augustine's body. Later, when Patricius spoke of it to

Monica, he joked about the promise of grandchildren. Augustine sums up what had disappointed him in his father: 'He saw in me only hollow things' (*Conf.* 2.3)

The relationship with his mother was one of the most vital things in Augustine's life. He admired and loved his mother. When he was born, she did not have him baptised. Instead, she made the sign of the cross on his forehead to claim him for Christ, and she put some salt on his tongue to preserve him from evil. However much he would, as a young man, pour scorn on her religion, he would always keep respect for the name of Jesus, which his mother had tried to instil into him. There was always a strong bond between him and Christ, and when he is converted he sees it as picking up the threads which he had let drop as a boy.

Monica was a woman of peace, and a peacemaker among her friends. He admires how she coped with a good but hot-tempered husband. How she had the sense not to argue with him, but to wait until he calmed down and then reason with him. Most of her friends bore the bruises of beatings by their husbands. Monica never did. Augustine admired too how she had borne with her husband's unfaithfulness over many years.

Augustine was a believer of sorts as a young boy. His mother would try to make up for the lack of faith in her husband's care of his son by encouraging him to choose God as his father. 'I was a believer like all my household, except father; but he could not cancel out in me the rights of my mother's godliness....for she tried earnestly, my God, that You should be my father, not him.' (*Conf.* 1.11) But it would be many years, and after many struggles, that Augustine would fully accept the faith that his mother tried to nurture in him.

Monica's 'godliness' meant that she was always deeply concerned about her son's spiritual well-being. She would never give up on her determination to see him become a Catholic. But she also had great ambitions for him to succeed in the world. Through his later turbulent years she would always have one eye on his prospects in the world of his career and one eye on the salvation of his soul.

From this family nest the young and clever boy emerged to try his wings in a world where success seemed certain. Away from the narrow little world of Thagaste he was on the path to a better life. He went to Madaurus at the age of twelve, to a school where he was certain to get the education that would open the door to a privileged career.

## 'I Hated School'

When it came to the discipline of study, the new pupil at Madaurus floundered. The system of education laid a crushing load on the memory. Though Augustine was eager to please, keen to succeed, he found his tasks boring and empty. Mathematics he found especially boring, Greek he stubbornly refused to study. He hated school. Above all he hated the beatings. Hated the humiliation of being given the lash. He tells us how he prayed to God to be spared the rod and was hurt that not only was his prayer not answered, but his parents even made a joke of the floggings.

However there was literature. He found that literature fired his imagination. He revelled in the classical tales of Rome. At the age of twelve he discovered Virgil. He wept for the fate of Dido, delighted in the tale of the wooden horse and the burning of Troy. The beauty of words, those 'precious cups of meaning' (*Conf.* 1.16) cast a spell on him. The Aeneid he would later know by heart. Poetry would always remain a treasure, and when he writes the story of his life, the language sings.

The education at Madaurus aimed to make the pupil a skilled user of words, 'a man who could give pleasure through his argument, by his liveliness, by the feelings at his command, by the ease with which words came to him, perfectly adapted to dress his message in style' (*Conf.* 5.6). These skills Augustine quickly mastered and he excelled in them for the rest of his life.

Madaurus was still a bastion of paganism, even though the Christian faith was steadily spreading all around. In such an environment the young boy would have found it hard to keep up the religious practices which his mother had taught him. He saw himself, as he later tells us, as a great sinner even in these early years. 'So small a boy and so great a sinner.' To escape work in order to play he lied to his teachers and masters. He stole from his parents, didn't play fair in games, and always wanted to be top in every competition. But, when he later looked back, he also gave himself credit for delighting in the truth, for hating to be deceived, for being gifted in speech, and for having a gift for friendship.

### A year of idleness

From his three years of schooling the teenage Augustine emerged as a gifted boy, eager to satisfy his parents' ambition and loving his chosen areas of study. But disaster hit when he was fifteen. His father could not meet the cost of the next year's school fees.

Augustine was doomed to spend a year of complete idleness back in Thagaste. He would, in later years, call this time the blackest period of his life.

It was during this year at home that, according to his own account, he fell into serious sin.

Chastity was not something to be valued in the society of his time, and Monica had to watch her little boy, now grown into a sturdy teenager, sow his wild oats. She lectured him, pointing out the evils of fornication and warning him especially against having affairs with married women. Augustine paid no heed. This was old women's talk, and he would be ashamed to pay any heed to it.

Casual affairs, an eagerness to match his friends in their sexual adventures, a yearning for love, this was the pattern of that troubled sixteenth year. 'All I wanted was to love and be loved.' (*Conf.* 2.2) But it was not the path of true love and friendship he trod. 'I did not keep within the bounds of an exchange between souls, wherein lies the luminous friendship.' Rather, he was 'pitched into the dark pools of lust'. The sexual excesses of this idle year were to form habits which he would struggle with for another fifteen years. The indulgences of this passionate year would shackle him and weaken his will, holding him bound and helpless, even when his mind was longing to follow the road that offered to lead him back to God.

### The pleasure of evil-doing

Another form of excess, a kind of 'fornication' of the soul, added to the dark memories of this black year. Near the vineyard belonging to Augustine's family stood a pear tree loaded with fruit. Late one night, in pursuit of mischief, Augustine and his gang ransacked the pear tree, ate a few of the tasteless pears, and threw the rest to the pigs.

This peccadillo troubled Augustine for many years. The senseless act of vandalism seemed more culpable than his sexual sins. Over and over again he asks why he took part in the pointless act of theft. It seemed to him to point to a deep sickness in his soul. 'Lord, let my heart tell you what it sought in that wrong doing, why it sought evil for evil's sake... ....I sought no profit from my evil-doing, simply the pleasure of the evil-doing itself.' (*Conf.* 2.4)

The wild year at home was not all disaster. The companionship he found in that year was the bright side to it. Friendship was becoming one of the great joys of his life. He would never be alone. He would always surround himself with friends. In his *Confessions* he writes these glowing words about the joys of friendship: 'to talk and to laugh, and to do each other kindnesses, to read pleasant books together; to pass the time in light or serious conversation: to argue without rancour, as one might dispute with oneself. The rare time we disagreed would only remind us of our usual harmony. To teach one another and learn from one another; to miss the absent and to long for their return; to welcome them back, happy to see them. Such were the signs of love, given and received, shown by looks and eyes and countless acts of kindness that warmed our lives and made us one.' (*Conf.* 4.10)

The idle year ended when his father had saved enough money to complete his education. His thrift and his hard work made it possible for his son to end this empty time between boyhood and manhood. Augustine, now seventeen, was ready to move on to university at Carthage, the third town of the Empire, after Rome and Constantinople.

Around this time, though it is hard to pinpoint the exact time, Patrick made his peace with his past and submitted himself to the Church. Monica's prayers for her husband's conversion, and her patience, were blessed. Patrick died without seeing any of his dreams for his son fulfilled. His death is barely mentioned in Augustine's *Confessions*.

## In Love with Love

The beautiful city of Carthage appealed to the teenage
Augustine as an exciting place for a young man in search
of love. 'I was not yet in love, though I was in love with
love; feeling a lack deep within me ....I sought something
to love, being in love with loving'. What he found was
not love, but a city seething with sexual excitement. The
habits of lax morals in which he had delighted in that
black year of idleness now flourished at Carthage. There
was no lack of opportunity for university youngsters,
often with too much time on their hands. 'I fell headlong
into the love with which I longed to be ensnared' (*Conf.*
3.1). The stormy love affairs of that first year at university
did not bring him the love he craved. He tells us how he
sought refuge at the theatre for his wounded heart. It was
the misery of separated lovers, the heartbreak of their
partings that fascinated him as a spectator.

His life of sensuality was not to be enjoyed without
some cost. He tells us how he suffered for the lack of any
restraint in his affairs with women. He felt 'the rods of
jealousy, suspicion, fear, anger and quarrelling'. When he
wrote about these years in his life's story, he was certain
that God was offering him a deeper love. He felt that God

was tugging at his heart. 'My God, with what bitterness did you season my pleasure!'

He would also see that in those years of amorous adventures he had confused love and sex and lust and friendship. And the great casualty, he felt, was friendship. 'The spring of friendship I sullied with the mire of lust.'*(Conf.* 3.1)

## The Wreckers

Another hang-over from the lazy year at home was the thrill he got from being a vandal. The mischief that he and his friends indulged in, 'especially after midnight', in Thagaste was carried over into his student days at Carthage. He joined a gang, called the 'wreckers', who got their thrills out of terrorizing staff and pupils at the university. Augustine was not at ease with the violent pranks of the gang, but he made sure that he belonged to it to stay with the in-crowd of his day (*Conf.* 3.3).

Despite the frolics, his studies were not neglected. He shone out as a star in his year. His future career was taking shape when it became clear that he was the best orator among his peers. The way his life was shaping promised success in law, the key to a secure career in the service of the Empire. His eyes would have been focussing on a lucrative post in the imperial civil service.

## The companion

But a change in his domestic life was to put a serious obstacle in the way. He met a young woman, apparently in church, and they set up house together. Her name we do not know. She was from a social class that would rule out marriage. He chose her, he tells us, 'because my sexual fancy had, in its ceaseless search, picked her out'. They were to live together for fifteen years. Augustine tells us that he was faithful to her for all that time. 'She was the only woman I had in those years.' (*Conf.* 4.2)

Soon she bore him a son. They had not wanted a child, but when he was born they named him 'Adeodatus', a name which means 'a gift from God'. Augustine was to love his son dearly and to admire his bright mind as he grew up.

Augustine had come to Carthage intending to cut a dash as an 'elegant and urbane' young man. But in setting up home with his mistress he had to be content with baby-minding and with domestic chores.

# 'An Unbelievable Fire in My Heart'

The years of casual love-making and of mischief-making came to an end when Augustine moved in with his mistress. He settled down to work earnestly and followed the course of studies that led directly to the profession of lawyer. In the course of his studies he read a book by Cicero that was to alter the direction of his life. It was an invitation to philosophy. It was Augustine's first taste of philosophy. It excited him. All his life he had a deep longing for truth: philosophy offered a new way of searching for truth, and for wisdom. From now on these would replace the pursuit of wealth and prestige as his goal in life. Philosophy, for centuries before Augustine's time, had been deeply linked with religion, and reading it brought him back to some of the truths he had learnt from his mother.

Augustine was enthralled by the promises made by philosophy, especially by the promise that Wisdom would help the divine part of him overcome the lusts of his body and the sly illusions of everyday life. 'I yearned for the immortality of wisdom and began now to arise that I might return to Thee, O my God.' His aim was not to pursue one or other school of philosophy, but to seek

Wisdom itself. 'To seek wisdom itself; to search for it; to pursue it, hold it, whatever it might be, was my burning ambition.' (*Conf.* 3.4)

Augustine was nineteen when he read Cicero, and it changed his whole outlook. 'This book changed all my feeling.... I was left with an unbelievable fire in my heart.' Augustine would never abandon the ideal of a life shaped by the love of wisdom. It would slip from view at times, but it had started him on a quest that he would never fail to follow.

He was 'swept along by this exciting prospect'. But there was one hesitation. There was no mention of Christ in the book. A pagan wisdom, a wisdom without a place for Christ, he could not accept. 'That name I had imbibed with my mother's milk, and I kept it deep within. And no book, however true or beautiful, could fully interest me, if the name of Christ were missing from it.' (*Conf.* 3.4)

What this experience did was to lead him back to the person of Christ, who had been at the centre of the religion he had been taught as a child. This set him to look seriously, for the first time, at the sources of the Christian faith. His hope was that he would find his 'Wisdom' there. It seems that he went first to the Old Testament. His first feelings were ones of disappointment.

He expected fine and polished language. The translations he read were in language that seemed to him crude when compared to the majesty of Cicero's writings.

What Augustine found seemed to him to compare badly with the beautiful spiritual wisdom that Cicero had invited him to love. He felt too that the historical books of the Old Testament were full of immoral and earthy stories. This disappointment made him look elsewhere for a truth and a wisdom that would make sense of his life.

It led him to a religion called Manichaeism. One of the things that attracted Augustine to this new religion was its rejection of the Old Testament as unspiritual and disgusting. This echoed his own feelings and made him easy prey to the overtures of the Manichees.

### Sidetracked from his quest

Augustine joined this new religion as a 'hearer'. He never joined the 'elite', who went in for severe fasting, complicated prayers and other austerities. Though Christ was a central figure for them, it was not the Christ of his childhood faith. The Manichees, as he later discovered, set traps for the unwary. They used the name of Christ as 'bird-catchers, who set their bird-lime at the edge of a pond to trap thirsty birds'. And the lime with which these traps were smeared was a 'mishmash of words, composed of the name of God, of our Lord Jesus Christ and of the Paraclete, our comforter, the Holy Spirit'.

What attracted him most was the friendship he was offered. He was seduced by the friendship and the cleverness of these well educated followers of Mani to accept what his mother would brand as 'heretical' teaching. And he remained with them for the next nine years. Augustine, not only accepted the teaching, but he was diligent in persuading many of his friends of earlier years to join, urging them to reject their Catholic faith and join his 'new' religion. They stood no chance against his astute mind and his skill with words. The Manichees regarded Catholics as half-baked Christians, and he got many pats on the back from his masters for his success in winning arguments against 'ignorant' Christians.

On the question of the origin of evil, which had deeply perplexed him for many years, the Manichees offered an answer that Augustine welcomed. 'I was feverishly looking for the origin of evil. What torments came from the travail of my heart!' The Manichees had an easy answer. God is good, they said, and evil exists independently of him. Evil could not come in any way from a good God. So they taught that the powers of Light and the powers of Darkness were co-equal. They were in permanent conflict, and would be until the end of time.

The idea of a power of evil at work in the world, independent of God, gave Augustine an easy explanation for sin. Some time after he joined the sect he wrote, 'It seemed to me that it is not we who sin, but I know not what strange nature within us...and I was happy to excuse myself by accusing some unknown "other" who was within me but not myself. (*Conf.* 5.18) This was a great comfort to him, excusing his sin and numbing his feelings of guilt, though not freeing him totally.

His excuse later for staying with the Manichees for so long was that he was certain that there was some deep secret in the teaching which would one day be revealed to him. He admired the austere lives of the 'Elect', he longed to imitate them in their practice of chastity, but he got no farther than praying for chastity. He prayed for it, but hoped that God would not answer his prayer too soon. 'Lord, give me chastity, but not just yet!' was his prayer.

He would soon leave the life of study and set out to earn his living in his home town, but he would retain links with the friends of his Manichee days. He was able to go on living with his partner without any objection from them, whereas if he were to pursue the path of true wisdom, or follow his mother's path, he would have to face painful decisions about his moral life.

## 'I Taught the Tricks of Speech'

Augustine's studies had prospered at Carthage. He took major prizes at public speaking contests, and was in the final year of his course when he and his mistress and young son returned to his home town. Until then, he and his little household had been supported by his mother and by the generosity of a wealthy patron whose help had rescued him after the disastrous year at home. It was time for him to earn his living. He had opted for a career in teaching rather than in law, and it was to teach that he came back to Thagaste.

It was a painful homecoming. Monica had seen her dreams for her talented son in ruins. Not only had he been sidetracked in his career prospects by taking a partner whom he could not marry, but he was the father of an illegitimate son. Most of all she was deeply hurt by his reneging on his Catholic faith. So, for the first and only time in her life, she refused to have him in her house.

However, she soon regained her better feelings for her son. Possibly she was charmed by the three-year-old grandson, Adeodatus, but also comforted by a dream she had had which seemed to promise that where she was her son would also be. She took this to mean that he would become a true Christian. She was also strengthened by the words of a bishop to whom she poured out her grief over what she saw as her son's spiritual death. The bishop said to her: 'it is impossible that the son over whom you have shed so many tears should be lost to God.' His advice to her was: 'Leave him alone for a while, and only pray to God for him.' (*Conf.* 3.12)

Back among his friends in his home town Augustine settled into the work of a teacher of rhetoric. The little town offered no prospects to a clever and ambitious young man, but life was pleasant and he was warmed by the presence of good friends. But fate took a hand in making his stay in Thagaste a short one. Tragedy struck in the death of a close friend. The two had bonded as children. On his return Augustine and he became the closest of friends. 'My soul could not do without him,' Augustine later wrote. The young man was a Catholic, but not strong in his faith, and he easily fell victim to the clever proselytizing of Augustine. He left his Catholic faith and became a Manichee.

Some months later this friendship – 'sweeter to me than all other sweetness in my life until then' - was shattered. The young man became ill and was unconscious, near death, and his Catholic family had him baptized. Augustine, staying at his bedside, was sure his friend would laugh at the superstitious precaution. When the friend got better, Augustine tried to joke about the baptism. He was astounded at the angry reply. If they were to remain friends, the young man said, there would be no more mockery about his being baptized. A few days later a relapse carried him off. Augustine was distraught. He felt he had lost his friend twice over. His death plunged Augustine into a pit of misery. Nowhere, perhaps, have better words been written that tell of the emptiness of a heart when a person who has been a soul's deepest friend is snatched from us by death. The loss of the friend had left him a 'stranger' to himself. It was as if he had been emptied of his deepest inner self. 'My native town was a torment, my home a strangely unhappy place. All the things we had done together, now that he was gone, became a daily torment. My eyes searched for him restlessly, but they did not see him. I hated all places because he was not in them.' (*Conf.* 4.4.)

He developed a loathing for Thagaste. The generous friend who had once before helped him to escape to a better life was the only one to whom Augustine spoke of his wanting to leave, and he offered to support him again, though he knew that his departure would deprive the town of a very gifted teacher. Augustine returned to Carthage to seek a better life, more ambitious than before, but also deeply troubled at heart.

## 'Time to Put My Soul Together Again'

Once he had returned to Carthage with his partner and young son, Augustine soon became known as a very uncommon teacher. He again threw himself into his studies, and by degrees his great sorrow eased. 'Time put my soul together again.'

He was barely four or five years older than his students, but his grasp of a wide variety of subjects, such as music, geometry and arithmetic, in addition to his skill at speaking and debating, made him an inspiration to many of his students. He seemed able to push them beyond the limits they would set themselves.

He found himself fascinated by astrology, and the attempts of his friends and of people in influential places to warn him of the dangers of becoming hooked on the divinations of astrologers failed to divert Augustine. The lure of astrology lasted many years. But even in this he was still in search of the wisdom that had first enthralled him at the age of nineteen when he read Cicero.

In the following nine years which he spent at Carthage he had many successes. He did not disappoint those who believed in him. He wrote his first book there, he won prizes in debating, and he was becoming known to the

Roman officials who held the high offices in the city. He had hopes of advancement.

In his quest for true wisdom he had put his trust in the religion of the Manichees. In his years at Carthage he grew disappointed with them. When nobody in the local group could help with his doubts, they fobbed him off by telling him to wait till Faustus came. Faustus, their great theologian, would answer his difficulties in the twinkling of an eye. Faustus came and proved a disappointment. He was eloquent, well-read, and impressive. But he knew no philosophy. He simply repeated the usual arguments, though in a more pleasing way. 'It was like a thirsty man being offered an empty cup of great value at the hands of a handsome cupbearer.' (*Conf.* 5.7)

This was an important moment in Augustine's spiritual journey. Though he did not abandon the Manichees, he was now waiting for a new guiding light. The let-down was probably one of the reasons why he decided to move to Rome. A beloved friend, Alypius, had moved to Rome. Various friends tempted him to follow, painting glowing pictures of high salaries and prospects of promotion. In later life Augustine would see the hand of Providence in all these invitations.

He had another reason for leaving Carthage. The rooms where he taught were in the centre of town. There was no protection from the gangs of unruly students who roamed about, intent on making mischief. His pupils were

mainly rowdy young fellows, sent from all over Africa by
their rich families to acquire a 'proper' education. 'They
would barge shamelessly into classrooms and destroy any
atmosphere of learning which the teacher might have
managed to create.' (*Conf.* 5.8) This, he would later say,
was the spur that made him decide to go to Rome.

Word from Rome was that the students were better
disciplined, so the decision was quickly made to cross the
sea to Italy. He made up his mind, but he did not escape
without strong opposition from the most important person
in his life.

# Rome: 'The Wind Rose and Filled Our Sails'

Before he could leave Africa for Rome, he had to deal with his mother's opposition. Monica had found out that he was leaving Carthage. Somehow she tracked him down to the seafront from where his boat was due to leave. She held on to him violently, begging him either to stay in Africa or to take her with him. He made her an excuse, saying that he had to go and say goodbye to a friend who was due to sail with the next favourable wind. Monica he despatched, against her will, to spend the night in a nearby shrine of St. Cyprian. 'I lied to my mother, a mother like her, and off I went.' As soon as she had gone, he took the next boat for Italy. 'The wind rose and filled our sail; the shore faded from our view.' It was a short crossing to Ostia. He went alone. His mother was left praying at the holy shrine. His partner and the young son were left behind to join him later.

In Rome he was welcomed by Manichaean friends to whom he had introductions. Almost as soon as he arrived, he became ill with an agonising fever. He felt he was facing death. Many years earlier, when he had been at the point of death, he had asked his mother for baptism, but it had not happened. Now, facing death for the second time, he did not feel the need for baptism. Though disillusioned with the faith of the Manichees, he was far from believing that the Catholic Church had the answer to his problems, or to his spiritual needs. He did, however, have faith in his mother's trusting prayers and, when he recovered, he felt that it was her pleas to God that had rescued him from danger.

He gathered around him a small number of students and quickly began to be known. He threw himself into his work. In Rome pupils did not disrupt lessons and did not play violent tricks on one another, or on the teacher. They had other and meaner faults. Near the end of term they would plot together and suddenly disappear, without paying their fees, and transfer to another teacher. He tired of their antics and began to look elsewhere for openings. The city itself did not work its magic on him and he had no desire to stay. It was overcrowded, and its sewers stank. He could leave it with no regrets.

Fortunately, his Manichaean friends had opened doors for him to some people of influence. Through them he met the high-ranking City Prefect. At the time when Augustine was having second thoughts about Rome the authorities in Milan, where the Emperor lived, had asked the Prefect to look out for someone to fill the post of Public Orator. Manichaean friends encouraged Augustine to apply, and they approached the Prefect on behalf of their protégé. Augustine applied and was asked to undergo a test. 'I submitted a trial speech to him,' he said later. 'He found it to his liking, and sent me to Milan.' (*Conf.* 5.23)

### 'To Milan I came, and to its bishop, Ambrose'

He moved to Milan on the eve of his thirtieth birthday. Here, in his post as Public Orator, he was on the public stage. It was a new life, mixing in a brilliant society, finding new interests, and with great chances of success. Soon after he arrived in the autumn of 384, he had to make a speech in praise of the boy-Emperor, Valentinian II. He felt awkward about heaping praise on a colourless adolescent; he worried about his African accent, and it didn't help, when on the way to make the speech, he came upon a happy drunk on the street. The drunk was so obviously content while Augustine, with his high ambitions, was not at ease with himself, or with the world. He managed the speech, he later wrote, 'by spouting a lot of lies, aimed to make the audience applaud, even though they weren't in the least fooled by the lies.' (*Conf.* 6.6)

Even though he was on the way to fulfilling his high ambitions, he was a troubled man. He had enjoyed the pleasures of youth. They had made him drunk with delight, but they had not satisfied his restless heart. He was craving for spiritual food. He had found wisdom in Cicero; he had, for a time, found companionship and a ready-made wisdom among the Manichees, and yet he was left disillusioned.

All his honours and successes were not bringing happiness. 'If good fortune smiled on me, I was too weary to lay hold of it; almost before I could get my hands on it, it was off in flight.' (*Conf.* 6.6) He would later say of that period of his life: 'At that time, there was no one more open to being taught than I was.' Fortunately, he was soon to meet someone who would become first a friend, and then his teacher. The man was Ambrose, bishop of Milan.

'That man of God gave me a fatherly welcome,' Augustine wrote of his first meeting with Ambrose. The bishop kept an open house. One did not need to be announced. The custom was for people to wander in and out, usually sitting while Ambrose, in a quiet corner of the room, was meditating or lost in silent reading. It wasn't the place for intimate discussion. 'It seemed unkind to interrupt. After we had sat a long time in silence, we would depart again.' (*Conf.* 6.3)

Even though he was very busy in those first weeks in Milan, Augustine found time to go and listen to Ambrose preaching, knowing that he was widely admired as one of the best of preachers. Curiosity drew Augustine. He was eager to listen to someone who was in the same profession and he was delighted by the eloquence of the bishop. At first it was the style of the orator that interested him. 'I made little effort to understand what Ambrose said, attending only to the style of the speaker.' (*Conf.* 5.13) But slowly the content of the sermons began to 'steal' into his mind. 'While my mind noted how eloquent his words were, my heart also noticed how true they were.' (*Conf.* 5.14)

What shook him most was Ambrose's way of dealing with Scripture. Ambrose managed to interpret the Prophets and the Laws in a spiritual sense. This helped wipe out of his mind the ideas of the Manichaeans that had so prejudiced him against the Old Testament. He was already on a new path. 'For now the things in the Scriptures which used to seem absurd are no longer so... ...I will set my foot on that step on which my parents placed me as a child, until I clearly find the truth.' (*Conf.* 6.11)

Listening to Ambrose also helped him shed some of his prejudices against the Catholic Church. He learned that he had been accusing the Church with blind obstinacy. 'I had not yet discovered that it taught the truth, but I now knew that it did not teach what I had so vehemently accused it of.' (*Conf.* 6.4)

The reasons he was reluctant to trust himself to the faith of Ambrose were very worldly reasons. They were far from intellectual. 'I was eagerly chasing after honours, money and matrimony. In pursuit of these ambitions I endured the most bitter hardships.' (*Conf.* 6.6) He did however value what he was learning about spiritual realities from the bishop and was grateful to him for wiping out of his mind what remained of his 'heretical' ideas.

## Monica's Return

Monica enters the story again at this juncture. She arrived from Africa along with the grandson, now a teenager, and his mother. Monica he had not seen since that night when he shamefully abandoned her on the beach at Carthage. He told her that, though he was no longer a Manichee, he was not yet ready to become a full Christian. He shared with her the respect he had for Ambrose, and this, he said, gave her hope. 'She loved that man, as if he were an angel of God, for she knew that it was he who led me to that state of doubt and wavering, through which, she had a sure intuitive feeling, I would have to pass in order to go from sickness to health.' (*Conf.* 6.1)

One thing that still prevented him from following the way opened up for him by Ambrose was his ambition and his thirst for honours. He was surrounded by influential friends; he was tasting the excitements of success. 'I longed for honours, gains, marriage.' He had come to Milan to fulfil his career ambitions. He had not lost sight of the path glimpsed twelve years earlier when he had resolved to follow the way of wisdom. Neither would Monica let him forget either his ambitions, or the spiritual path he had chosen.

There was one obstacle to his high ambition, which had to be faced urgently. The way to further success would be blocked to him were he to marry his mistress. Sadly, in the culture of the Roman world in which he hoped to advance, no marriage was possible. As he would later tell it, the woman who had shared his bed for sixteen years had become an obstacle to his career. Roman law forbad marriage between people of different social classes. Augustine had to face the terrible choice, either to separate from his mistress, or give up on his hopes of further advancement. He was under pressure to part with the woman who had supported him for all these years and who had borne him a precious son. The heartbreaking decision was made to send his mistress back to Africa. She went, but she left vowing to know no other man in the future. She also had to part with her son, who remained with his father.

## 'I Became More Unhappy, But You More Near'

At this moment of his life Augustine's spiritual state was at its bleakest. He had come to Milan to seek honour and wealth. He still eagerly wanted to follow the path opened up for him when he had read the invitation to pursue wisdom. He had prospects of a brilliant career. But the way forward had meant the sacrifice of the woman he loved.

'Since she was an obstacle to my marriage, the woman I lived with for so long was torn out of my side. My heart was rent and wounded; it bled.' (*Conf.* 6.15)

Augustine was deeply divided and unhappy. He was haunted by thoughts of success in his career. He had proved that he was not in control of his sexual drives. He had been guilty of treachery to the woman he loved. And he was still torn by religious doubts. But as he later reflected the unhappiness, strangely, brought God nearer. 'The more unhappy I grew,' he later wrote, 'the closer you came.' (*Conf.* 6.16) He did not excuse himself for his betrayal, or for his weaknesses, but he was aware that God was holding out a hand to him.

His religious doubts were many. He preferred the Catholic Church to any other creed, but he was still confused by the problem of evil, for which no one had provided him with a convincing explanation. He felt that, were he to become a full Catholic, he would have to cease from craving after worldly success. An even greater question was whether, if he presented himself to the Divine Physician, he would have to surrender the sensual pleasures without which he could not live. To become a Christian like Ambrose would involve, he believed, giving himself totally. Chastity was the biggest obstacle to his giving himself to the Christian life. He felt that he would be miserable 'unless he was enfolded in the arms of a woman.' (*Conf.* 6.11)

The answer for the moment was to find someone suitable for him to marry. So Monica set about finding him a wife. She had no choice. He loudly proclaimed that he could not live without the embraces of a woman. She longed for his happiness; she put great store on his success, but she longed, most of all, for his soul's salvation. Hers was an impossible dilemma.

### 'I wooed. I became engaged'

Monica found a young woman of a rich family. Augustine was introduced and liked her enough to agree to an engagement. 'I wooed. I became engaged, mostly thanks to my mother's efforts.' (*Conf.* 6.13) The young woman was two years under the legal age for marriage, so they decided to wait. He vowed that, until the two years were up, he would live without the embraces of a woman. This vow lasted only a very short time. To his shame he found he was unable to abstain. He took a mistress to fill the void.

The little group of friends he had drawn round him at Milan were on hand to offer him support and comfort at this time of desolation. The friendship among them was balm to his warm nature. They also brought God closer. Looking back, Augustine would realise how many avenues God would travel to meet him.

### 'I was led astray by the mists of a befouled heart'

A great deal was happening in his life at this, the end of his first year in Milan. His success in his career was remarkable, he was engaged to be married, so, socially, everything was promising. Yet his heart was in turmoil. He was, he said, 'led astray by the mists of a befouled heart.'

It was at this point of turmoil and unhappiness that Augustine had an experience in which he later saw the hand of God clearly at work. A friend lent him some books. These were his first encounter with the philosophy of the Platonists, a school of philosophy which was most influential from the third to the sixth century. These books were to bring about a profound change in his thought. 'You provided for me some books of the Platonists, translated from Greek into Latin.' (*Conf.* 7.9) The encounter with this new philosophy was the first of several dramatic meetings that were to bring Augustine to the brink of conversion.

Among the key ideas which the Platonists taught were; 'We need but recollect ourselves and remember that we are Gods, and already we are Gods. Hence our effort must always be directed at purgation, at ridding ourselves as far as possible of the Matter which is the clothing of our decay, and to asserting the Godhead in us, until we are altogether freed from the body and resume our union with the One, or, as he is sometimes called, the Father.' (O'Meara *The Young Augustine*, p. 130)

The invitation was to enter into the depths of one's own being. Wisdom comes from the knowledge of self, and that happiness is to be found by obeying the ancient command: 'Know yourself'. The key to wisdom was to 'return to yourself'. This teaching, that the soul becomes truly rich by discovering its true self, greatly attracted Augustine. It set his heart on fire, even more than the reading of Cicero had done twelve years earlier. The life of a human being, it taught, should be a gradual liberation from the fetters of this life and should be an ascent to God.

### 'With you as guide I entered my deepest self'

Augustine's debt to this new thinking is described briefly in his *Confessions*. 'These books helped me to return to myself. With you as guide, I entered my deepest self. I entered into myself, and with the eyes of my soul I saw the Light within... All who know the truth see this light, and all who see this light see Eternity. It is the light that Love knows.' (*Conf.* 7.10) Only a little time earlier Augustine had been weighed down by desolation. Now he found his mind bathed in new light, a light more satisfying than the light that had shone for him when he read philosophy as a student. These books had much in common with Christian teaching, and to Augustine's delight he discovered that Ambrose, in his preaching, often quoted from them. His soul was on fire once again. In his new state of excitement he felt that he had found the real path to wisdom, and that path was the inward path that led him to the depths of his own soul.

# 'I Withdrew Completely Into Myself'

The startling discovery then was that truth was to be found within oneself. 'I entered my innermost being led by your guidance.' (*Conf.* 7.16) And in that journey he found the light of God within himself. This light sharply brought home to him what a distance there was between him and God. 'You struck my feeble gaze with the power of your beams of light, and I found myself to be far from you.'

There was, however, a weakness in the books he was reading that jarred on him. It was the same as the one he had noticed in Cicero. There was no mention of Christ. Even though, at this point, Augustine's understanding of Christ was flimsy, he still had great regard for the name of Jesus. His notion of Christ was of a human being, far above the rest of humanity, a man of eminent wisdom, who was sent to the world as an example of despising earthly things for the sake of achieving eternal life.

The absence of any mention of Christ in these books sent him to the writings of St. Paul. He read the epistles with great enthusiasm. Here he found that the eloquence of the apostle dispersed many of his false ideas about Christ. He found that his doubts were dissolving. He was on the way to seeing the truth of the faith, in which he had been nurtured, but which he had scorned in his troubled years.

His mind was convinced, but the moral difficulties remained. The thoughts of worldly success had begun to fade. They no longer had the power to tempt him. But the seductive attractions of the love of women held his will bound. (*Conf.* 8.1) The cost of following Christ seemed too great. 'The Way, our Saviour himself, delighted me, but the narrow path I was as yet loath to follow.' (*Conf.* 8.1)

## Three remarkable stories

Augustine had a friend, an old priest, who had helped him when he was wrestling with the ideas of the Platonists. This kind old man had earlier eased Augustine's doubts by telling him that, while other philosophies were full of lies and deceit, the books he was reading were full of intimations of God and his Word. When his inner turmoil was becoming too much for him, it was to this priest that he poured out his heart. 'I hoped that if I unburdened myself to him he would show me how best someone like me might walk your way.' (*Conf.* 8.1)

The old priest related to him the remarkable story of the man who had translated the books in which Augustine was delighting. The name of the man, Victorinus, was well known to Augustine; the story of his conversion to the Christian faith he had not heard. This man had held high office in Rome, and was everywhere respected. When he wanted to convert to the Catholic faith, the Roman clergy offered to let him do it in private to save such an eminent person embarrassment. But he chose a public confession. At the time, a time of persecution by Julian the Apostate, Christians were not allowed to teach literature or oratory, so he chose to step down from office and resign his chair at the university.

### 'I was on fire to imitate him'

The story moved Augustine. He admired the man's courage and longed to be able to give himself totally to the Catholic faith! 'The moment he told me about him I was on fire to imitate him.' (*Conf.* 8.10) Augustine's mind was won over, but his heart still clung to the old joys. 'The enemy had seized my will, and of it made a chain to bind me. My will was perverse. It had turned to lust, and lust became habit, and habit, not resisted, became necessity.' (*Conf.* 8.5)

The story of the conversion of one of Rome's leading figures had inspired him, but his heart and will were still in revolt. He began, nonetheless, to feel a new attraction. 'A new will was beginning to stir within me, the will to enjoy you, my God. This will was not yet strong enough to win over the old will, hardened by custom. So within me were two wills, one under the power of the flesh, the other spiritual. They were in conflict, and the conflict tore me apart.' (*Conf.* 8.5)

## The longest day

Two other stories told to him soon after offered an even greater challenge. One was the story of the hermit, Anthony, and the other a story of two members of the Emperor's bodyguard who had left their careers and their fiancées and become members of a hermit community.

The stories came from an officer in the secret police, an African and a Christian, who dropped in one afternoon to visit Augustine in the villa outside Milan where he and his friends were staying. Only Augustine and Alypius were at home. The visitor idly picked up a book which was lying on a table, assuming that it would be one of Augustine's textbooks. He was surprised to find it was the letters of St Paul. Somehow, the visitor found himself relating the story of St. Anthony, the Egyptian monk. Anthony had spent his life in a hermit's cave, and his example was causing young people all over the Empire to leave the glittering world of power and pleasure and follow the hermit vocation.

Augustine and Alypius had not previously heard the story, and listened 'in silent attention'. That such stories were becoming everyday news was astonishing. More astonishing was the fact that just outside Milan's city walls there was a flourishing Christian community of young men, and that Augustine had never heard of it. The visitor then went on to relate a tale from his own experience which was to make the ground shake under Augustine's feet.

Some years earlier, when he was serving at Trier, in the Emperor's entourage, while his master was enjoying an afternoon at the circus games, he went for a walk with three comrades in the gardens outside the city walls. The little group had split into pairs. While he and his companion wandered on their path, the other two came upon a house where some hermits were living. There they found a book telling the story of Anthony's life. They sat down to read it. One of the two was so inspired by it that he said to his companion: 'Where is our work leading us to? What more can we hope for, after going through many pains and dangers, than to be 'friends of the emperor', whereas to be 'the friend of God', if I so want it, can be achieved this instant?'

They did not hesitate for long. When the other two rejoined them, the two friends had made a decision. In that moment of questioning they had decided to leave everything and stay with the community of hermits. The story ended with the sad reflection that the man who related the story, and his companion, returned to the imperial palace 'their hearts heavy with the cares of the world'.

## The garden

No sooner had the story finished than Augustine turned to Alypius and in a state of turmoil said: 'What is the matter with us? What is the meaning of this story? These men have none of our education, yet they stand up and storm the gates of heaven while we, with our knowledge and no heart, do nothing but wallow in flesh and blood.'

Augustine, in his torment, broke away and went to the bottom of the little garden where he and Alypius used to seek solitude. Alone with himself he faced the division in his soul. His anguish, he wrote later, turned into deep anger. 'I was distraught, seething with deep anger against myself for not following your way, or yielding to your will, my God.'

Alypius watched from a little distance as Augustine's torment threw him into uncontrolled rage. Augustine's later recorded those moments. 'I tore at my hair, I pounded on my forehead with my fists, I locked my fingers and clasped my knees.'

He felt that what was holding him back was the lure of trivial things. 'Trifles held me back, insignificant trifles. Empty toys, my old friends, pulled at my garments and whispered, "are you sending us away?"' and, "will we from this moment never again have a place in your life?" And, "from this moment will this or that never ever be allowed again?"

On the other side chastity beckoned. 'On that side I saw continence, a peaceful, inviting presence gently enticing me to cross over and to be unafraid, and stretching out hands ready to welcome me and to hold me.' He saw too 'many, many people, boys and girls young folk, people of every age, older people who all had lived lives of continence. In the midst the figure of Continence, not childless, but a mother of countless children, the children of joy, children, Lord, born of you.'

Overwhelmed by a storm of tears, he got up and moved away from his friend, 'so that I might weep to my heart's content'. He flung himself under a fig tree and let the tears flow. He found himself saying over and over 'How long? How long will I go on saying "tomorrow and tomorrow?" Why not now? Why not in this very moment end my wretchedness?'

Suddenly, he heard a voice from a neighbouring house, a voice, it seemed, of a little boy or girl, repeating, repeating, 'Take and read, take and read'. He stopped weeping. He intently searched his memory, trying to think 'if there was any game where children used this refrain'. But never before did he remember hearing such words. He got up, sure that this was a command from God to open the book of the Scriptures and read the first passage he might find. He rushed back to where he had dropped the book of Paul's letters. He grabbed it, opened it, and in silence read the first lines on which his eyes fell:

'Not in revelling and drunkenness, not in debauchery and licentiousness, not in quarrelling and jealousy; instead put on the Lord Jesus Christ; forget about satisfying your bodies with all their cravings.' (*Rom* 13:13-14)

He didn't wish to read further. There was no need. 'For, in an instant, as I came to the end of the sentence, it was as if a light of confidence flooded my heart and the dark shadows of doubt were dispelled.' Of all the passages in Paul's letters which he could have stumbled upon in that blind rush to open the book, this was the one that carried the strongest message for him. Of all the things that had stood in his way to the perfect life which he so longed for, it was not ambition or the lure of wealth or fame that had been the biggest barrier, but what Paul calls 'the satisfaction of the flesh and its lusts'. And he could not help seeing it as a little miracle that it was this verse, above all, from the Letter to the Romans that he stumbled on at the right moment.

As soon as he had marked the place and closed the book, he went in search of Alypius and told him everything that had happened. Alypius asked to see the passage. Going on some lines further he found the words, 'him that is weak in faith, receive him'. These words Alypius applied to himself, and in that moment he, too, found the strength to take the leap into faith. Together they went to tell Monica. She was overwhelmed with joy and thanked God that his answer to her longings and her prayers had been so much more wonderful than she could ever have hoped for. Her son had not only found faith, but had chosen to follow his Lord in a more wholehearted way than she could ever have foreseen.

Twelve or so years later, when he wrote his *Confessions*, Augustine found himself trying to trace God's hand in the process of his conversion and of his life. The question he asked was not where was God during his years of wandering and misery, but where was he himself during those years. He lamented his blindness, his deafness. He realized that God was never absent. God was with him. But he was not with himself. He was absent, he was living outside himself. This is his lament: 'Late have I loved you; late have I loved you. You were with me, but I was outside myself. There I sought you, rushing about among the beautiful things you had made. You were with me, but I was not with you.'

In finding God he had also found himself. It was in the depths of his own heart that he found what he had spent long years looking for. He found God in the centre of his life, and ever after he would encourage his hearers and readers that, if they were searching for God, they should return to their own hearts.

# Time to be Still

Decisions were quickly made. Augustine would resign his post as Milan's professor of rhetoric, 'gently to withdraw the service of my tongue from the chatter market,' as he puts it. He and his family and friends would then seek a place in the country to be quiet and rest. Fortunately, Augustine had a good excuse for taking retirement. His health in previous months had been a cause of worry. Breathing problems, chest pains, difficulty in speaking for any length, all offered the excuse which would let him escape without notice.

It was August 386, just before the summer break at the university where he taught. He got through the last few weeks of term and then with a group of close friends, including his mother, his brother, his son, Alypius, and others, he accepted an offer from a good friend of a villa, situated north of Milan, in the foothills of the Alps.

Here, in the quiet of the country, the group set up a little community. In a life of prayer, discussion and work on the grape harvest, living a life of friendship, Augustine and his family and friends enjoyed a long retreat. In that time of rest he and his friends had dialogues about the questions that had been occupying his mind for years. There was, above all, time for Augustine to find his way in the new relationship with God. And time for long discussions about the issues of faith that had not yet been explored.

Questions about truth, about beauty, about happiness, about order, and many other topics occupied the group at all hours, indoors and outdoors, and afterwards they wrote up their findings, or, rather, Augustine turned all these wonderful exchanges into books. Away from the turmoil he had been through, free from the bustle and from the loud, boisterous life with his students, he was able to enjoy the leisure which he saw as sacred. Almost his first instinct after that moment of conversion was, he said, to find time to be still and, in the stillness, see God. (*Psalm* 46) In the villa where he and his group of friends rested Augustine found that the days were not long enough to explore all the questions that he wanted to delve into, and to deepen his knowledge of God and of himself. 'Make me know myself, make me know you' was his constant prayer.

### 'We left the country and went back to Milan'

Winter passed, and the group returned to Milan. Augustine and Alypius needed to enrol for baptism. Throughout the spring of 387 they went through a demanding course of preparation, which included fasting, penance and instruction. He would later recall how he spent those weeks being 'catechized, exorcized and examined'. Yet he still found time for more writing.

At the Easter Vigil, on the night of 24-25 April, 387, Augustine, Alypius and his son Adeodatus were baptised by Bishop Ambrose. They went down into the baptismal font, were totally immersed in the cleansing waters, and came out to be clothed in a white tunic, a symbol of the new person whose sins lay on the pavement, with the old clothes they had left behind before they entered the pool. Of that night Augustine writes simply: 'And we were baptised, and the turmoil of our past life fled from us'. (*Conf.* 9.14)

The days that followed were days of celebration, of sheer happiness. 'How I wept to hear your hymns and canticles, greatly moved by the voices whose melody resounded in your church! Those voices flowed into my ears, and the truth was distilled in my heart; and all was well with me' (*Conf.* 9.6). It was, he later wrote, 'as though, after I had so long sighed for your fragrance, I could at last breathe it in, at least in so far as human frailty can perceive it' (*Conf.* 9.7). Giving himself to God involved not only being changed in mind and will to loving God, but being caught up totally, in body and affections as well, into the delight which is God. 'God is delight', he writes, 'and we rest in delight with him'.

It was soon time to move on. Augustine no longer had a life, or an income, in Milan. He had had two years of dazzling success there, he had had glowing prospects before him, but he set these aside, once the great tribulations of mind and heart had finally been put to rest. He decided to return to his homeland, hoping to find some place where he and the others might be most useful in God's service.

## Monica's Death

The little group travelled down to Rome and stopped at Ostia. There they rested before taking the boat to North Africa. It was there, in a quiet dwelling, overlooking a garden, that Augustine and his mother had a kind of vision of eternity that lifted their souls to the precincts of heaven. It was this experience that taught Augustine a truth that was to influence so much of his thought, that inward silence is the condition for pure, direct communion with God.

It was there at Ostia that, some days later, Monica died. She had been ill for nine days. Her sense that she was going to die there prompted her to say that she didn't mind where they buried her, provided they remembered to pray for her at the Eucharist. 'Nothing,' she said, 'is far from God, and I need not fear that at the end of the world he will not know where to find me to raise me up.' (*Conf.* 9.28)

Augustine closed Monica's eyes and though, he later said, 'a great wave of sorrow surged into my heart,' he restrained his tears in public. He felt that no tears were needed for someone who had died in his mother's state. He kept back the tears again when the body was carried out for burial, even though he was secretly weeping within. A night's sleep helped to relieve the sorrow a little, but soon the tears that he had been holding back streamed down. 'I let them flow as freely as they would, making of them a pillow for my heart.' (*Conf.* 9.12)

Leaving Monica's body buried at Ostia, the band of heartbroken friends set out for Africa. But it was too late for sailing. Winter had come, so they set up home for about ten months in Rome. Here Augustine saw the city as if for the first time. He discovered the great treasures of Christian history, which had held no interest for him when he lived there.

## Community at Thagaste

In the autumn of 388, when he saw the coast of Africa, Augustine was a very different man from the person he was when he left it five years earlier. His ambition now was to live, along with his close friends, a life totally dedicated to God's Word. He resolved to set up a little community in his home town. The family home was there to live in, and there he set himself to follow his dream of living a contemplative life in a Christian setting.

He had learnt from the Platonists how to withdraw into his innermost self, how to find a pleasant dwelling place in his own heart. Now he sought that way as the surest way of reaching God. The time at Thagaste was a wonderfully creative time. The community setting enabled Augustine to continue his dialogue with his friends. Out of those dialogues came several books. Adeodatus was in his late teens now and he took his full part in the discussions. He showed extraordinary promise. But he was not to live to fulfil that promise. We are not sure when, but, before he reached his twentieth year, he died. Augustine found strength from his new faith not to grieve excessively, but later in life, in his last book, there is a sentence that is taken to refer to Adeodatus: 'Of all people, you are the only one I would wish to surpass me in everything.' (*De gratia et libero arbitrio* 45)

### Seized and dragged into the bishop's presence

Life in the community at Thagaste, where he lived his dream, was not to last long. His books and his name began to be known, drawing more attention to him than he wanted. He was aware of the common practice by which the local church, when they saw a suitable candidate, would choose someone to be their bishop, even against the candidate's will. Augustine took care to avoid places where the bishop's chair was vacant. He had no fears when he went to church in the neighbouring city of Hippo. On one visit to see a friend he set out to look for a suitable site to set up a monastic community. He attended church, at ease with himself, since the city had a bishop.

But the bishop was an old man, a mediocre speaker, and in the course of his sermon he told his hearers that he needed a helper. There was a shout from the congregation. Augustine was recognized, surrounded, and dragged into the bishop's presence. There he was straightaway ordained. Bewildered, and overcome with guilt because of his past, he broke into tears. Looking back on that moment he later wrote: 'Terrified by my sins and the weight of my misery, I had resolved in my heart, and meditated fleeing into solitude; but you prevented me and I put all my cares into your hands, O Lord, for as long as I live.' (*Conf.* 10.43) The dream of living in a sheltered community, with ample time for 'the one thing necessary' (*Lk* 10.32), a life of contemplation and study, but also at the service of others, was shattered. As a priest he would be at the service of his bishop.

Augustine wrote to the bishop asking for leave for study and prayer. He was allowed a few weeks, and after this brief time of preparation he went straight into the work which the tired bishop wanted most help with, the breaking of the Word of God to the fishermen and their families, who comprised his new audience. His dream of living in community was not completely lost. Even though most of his days would be given to the work of his priesthood, the bishop gave him a house with a garden, close by the cathedral.

Here, in Hippo, he would live for the rest of his life, which was almost for forty years.

## 'All Must be Loved'

Augustine was clear about his calling as a priest. He expressed it in these words: 'to render an account to the Prince of all shepherds of the flocks who may be entrusted to me' (*Letter* 23). He now placed at the service of the Church the gifts and skills he had used with such success in his life as teacher of public speaking. Among the tasks he soon faced was the battle with his old 'heretical' friends, the Manichees. He was as eager now to destroy their influence as he once was to promote it. He was especially keen to rescue those whom he had once drawn into error.

The leaders of the wider Church saw how talented he was and put him to work at Church regional councils. They delighted in promoting the young priest who, they saw, was a genius in the use of words, the like of whom Africa had not known for a very long time.

In his pastoral work he battled with the abuses that defiled the feasts of the martyrs, the drunken revellings that were so common. He had to use all his eloquence to restore discipline. There were divisions in the Church, springing from dangerous splinter groups. He would spend a great part of his life fighting these deep divisions. To equip himself better for his tasks he went back to studying the Scriptures and writing his own reflections on them. He spent his days at his pastoral tasks, his nights immersed in his studies and his writing.

Soon, when a bishop was needed in the surrounding dioceses, eyes were cast on Augustine. His bishop, Valerius, knew what a treasure he had in his young priest and, once, when there was a concerted move made to take Augustine away from him, he hid him away in a secret place. Valerius decided that the only way to keep Augustine was to ask the higher authorities to appoint him as co-bishop. This was agreed to, and at the age of forty, Augustine was ordained a bishop. We have his own words to tell us how he saw the tasks of one who is trusted with the care of souls: 'The turbulent have to be corrected, the faint-hearted cheered up, the weak supported; the Gospel's opponents need to be refuted, its insidious enemies guarded against; the unlearned taught, the indolent stirred up, the argumentative checked; the proud must be put in their place, the desperate set on their feet, those engaged in quarrels reconciled; the needy have to be helped, the oppressed to be liberated, the good to be encouraged; the bad to be tolerated; all must be loved.' (*Sermon* 340)

It became very clear to him, especially when Bishop Valerius died and Augustine had to take on the responsibilities on his own, that the struggle with the 'insidious enemies' of the Church would be long-running and certainly no easy job. He still longed for the support of life lived in community, so he moved into the bishop's house from the monastery in the gardens where he had lived. Here he set up a new community of the clerics with whom he worked. He continued to live the life of prayer and reflection and community as much as his busy life would allow.

### 'He worked by day and watched by night

Thus was set up the pattern of life he followed for nearly forty years. His fame as a preacher and teacher spread all over North Africa. He was in demand everywhere and travelled widely in his role as the Church's most accomplished defender against the many 'opponents of the Gospel'. He was tireless in trying to make peace among the warring factions. Yet he found time to write his books, among them his most important work, *The Confessions*, along with the huge books *On the Trinity* and *On the City of God*.

Nor were all his works written for the learned. He could also write simple books for the ordinary people, like his *Instructions for Beginners* and *How to Teach the Faith to the Illiterate*. Everywhere he went he was accompanied by people who would take down in shorthand what he said, and later his secretaries would make copies. His sermons, of which about four hundred (a tenth of his output) survive, were faithfully recorded by his secretaries.

People wrote to him from France, from Italy, from Jerusalem, from all over the Roman world. His responses survive, and we get from them the feel of his life as he lived it. We wonder how he could hold together the many duties and responsibilities - his pastoral work, his preaching, his work in Church councils, his writing, his debates with the enemies of the Church - and yet find time for prayer and community. His biographer attempts to answer that question: 'After he had put aside the tasks of administration, he turned his mind to the realities of the inner life. He meditated, seeking divine truth. Then he had his secretaries record what he had learnt in his meditation. He always corrected what he had written or dictated. In order to do all this he worked by day and watched by night'.

He never lost his yearning for the life of contemplation. It was not easy to set aside time for it, and we get a glimpse of his longing in a little book, called *The Work of Monks*.

One of the most draining tasks of a bishop in those days was that he was a judge in disputes. Augustine did not shy away from the work, which he found engrossing. But he tells his readers how much he misses the life of the monastery. 'When it comes to my own creature comforts, I would much more prefer to do some manual work at set times, and take advantage of the other moments to read, pray, or study the holy Scriptures, than to be exposed to the stormy complexities of other people's squabbles in secular affairs.' (*The Work of Monks*, 37)

In one of his sermons he speaks about the daily frustrations he faced in his work as a judge. He tells of the humiliations he endured when he tried to get justice done for his flock with the secular powers. He relates how he would wait in the ante-chamber of the bureaucrats he was meeting, obliged to watch others being ushered in before him without their having to wait. More often than not he had to accept refusals and rebuffs rather than getting a satisfactory answer. Then, the most mortifying thing of all, when his appeal failed, he had to endure the ingratitude of those for whom he had worked. Frequently, they showed that they had doubted whether he had done anything at all!

## The final years

One of the things that clouded his life in his later years was the increase in the slave trade. In a letter he wrote to his dear friend Alypius, who by then was also a bishop, he wrote of his anguish at the lack of action by the public authorities to stem the trade. He relates how hired men dressed up as soldiers went 'in howling bands' through the country villages. Choosing remote areas they would burst into villages during the night, killing the men and taking off the women and children to sell. One can tell from the letter how overwhelmed with horror Augustine was and how weary he was becoming.

In spite of his weariness he continued to fight in every way open to him for the unity of the Church. He continued to preach, to teach, to write, to travel. The toll on his health eventually made him seek the approval of his clergy and his congregation to appoint someone to succeed him. The assembly he called approved of his choice. The new man would take over only at Augustine's death. In the meantime, Augustine was able to offload on to him the heaviest of his responsibilities.

From then on he returned to the life he had had to forego when he was ordained priest, a life in which prayer and study took priority. He set aside five days a week for his studies of the Scriptures. Lest anyone think he was idle, he let his flock know that he was not wasting his time: 'Let no one envy me this leisure time, for it is well and truly occupied.' (Letter 213) Part of this 'leisure' time he gave to the monumental task of revising all his writings. He was able too to devote time to 'the one thing necessary,' the enjoyment of being in God's presence in silence.

Thus, one of his final lessons to his followers was to assert the importance of balance in their lives. This balance is meant to apply to all followers of the Gospel. Augustine spoke of three kinds of life. The contemplative, which was the life Mary of Bethany found by sitting at the feet of Jesus; the active, which is busy with human affairs;

and the mixed, which combines both of these. Augustine wants his followers to live the mixed life, a life of contemplation, out of which flows the life of attention to the needs of others. He writes: 'No one should be so at leisure as in their leisure not to think of their neighbour's needs; nor so busy as not to seek after the contemplation of God,' (*The City of God*, xix) His hope is that we do not let ourselves 'abandon the delight of contemplation, lest the sweetness of it be withdrawn from us, and the tasks we have to undertake overwhelm us. In one of his letters he exhorted a community of monks to hold fast to their manner of life, but to be available if the Church should need them: 'Do not', he wrote, 'prefer your own leisure to the needs of the Church.' (*Letter* 48)

### The miracle on his death-bed

Over the final years of his life there was a great cloud. The Vandals overran the Empire.

An army of 80,000 crossed from Spain and landed in North Africa. Soon they were at the gates of Hippo. Augustine stayed at his post. A long siege started and, in the third month of it, he fell ill. Attacked by fever he retired to his room, where he asked not to be disturbed, except at mealtimes, or when the doctor called. One day a person who was seriously ill called, with a relative, and insisted on seeing the bishop. They begged that Augustine should lay hands on the sick person. The reply from

Augustine was that if he had such power he would be the first to take advantage of it himself. The visitor persisted, saying that he had been told in a dream to go and see the bishop to be cured. Augustine laid hands on the man, and he went away healed.

During his final illness the psalms dealing with penitence had been copied at his request and placed on the walls so that he could read them from his bed. On August 28, in the year 430, Augustine died. He had lived almost seventy-six years, forty of them as priest or bishop. The siege of Hippo lasted fourteen months, and, at the end of it, the town was burned to the ground, all its inhabitants having fled. The Dark Ages had come.

Tradition has it that Augustine's vast library was saved and sent to Rome. It is reckoned that his output amounts to over five million words. Someone has said that if anyone claims to have read the whole of Augustine's writings, they are probably lying!

Less than a year after Augustine's death, Pope Celestine wrote: 'We have ever regarded Augustine as a man of saintly memory. We have long known him as a man of such learning that he was always regarded by our predecessors as one of the greatest of doctors.' On the apse of St. Peter's Basilica in Rome, under the Gloria of Bernini, the chair of Peter is supported by four massive figures, the greatest doctors of the Church. One of them is Augustine of Hippo.

Almost from the time he died Augustine has been the dominant figure in the thought of Christian Europe. He is mentioned in the manuscripts of every century. He has been at the centre of many disputes. He has had many critics and has been blamed for what those who criticize him see as intolerance and narrow-mindedness. Yet he continues to offer wise and beautiful teaching to all who have ears to hear. His story, as related in the *Confessions*, has spoken to people of every time and country.

Among all the things he has written or said, one sentence has been quoted more often than any other. It is from the first paragraph of the first chapter of his *Confessions*. 'You have so made us, Lord, that we long for you, and our heart is restless until it rests in you.'

One of the truths that we most need to learn from Augustine is this: that we will find no happiness until our hearts rest in God. To rest in God is to be at peace, to be free of worry, free of anxiety about the future. To rest in God means to bring mind and heart into a state of quietness. If we do that, he tells us, we 'shall see into eternity'.

Augustine's idea of God is very different from the popular notions of God. His idea is of a God who brings rest to our troubled hearts. 'God is delight and we rest in delight with him, called home from the noise that is around us to the joys that are silent.'

When he writes his life story, he does not ask where God was during the long years of his wandering. He realizes that God was always with him, but he sees clearly that he was not with God. He was 'outside' himself, rushing about among the beautiful things God had made. He had become a stranger to himself, and until he found himself he could not find God.

I leave you with one of the most moving passages in *The Confessions*. It captures more beautifully than anything I have read in Christian literature the loving tenderness of the heart of our God.

Looking back on his life Augustine saw that long before he accepted Christ and his gospel he was being led into a place of quietness. God had been enveloping him in his love, drawing him, unawares, into his embrace. He is using the same image which Jesus used when he lamented the refusal of the people of Jerusalem to accept his loving protection, the image of the little chicks being gathered under the mother's wings. (*Matthew* 23:37)

Augustine wrote: 'Unknown to me you caressed my head. You closed my eyes lest they see the things that kept me from you. I lost for a while the heavy burden of self and my madness was lulled to sleep. And when I awoke in you I saw you as utterly different.' (*Conf.* 7.14)

# Prayers and Reflections by St Augustine

God is delight
and we rest in delight with Him,
called home from the noise that is around us
to the joys that are silent.
Why do we rush about
to the top of heaven
and the bottom of earth
looking for Him
who is here at home with us,
if only we could be
with Him?

∞

Surrender to Him
what you have,
since all came from Him.

∞

You made us
so that we long for You,
and our hearts are restless
until they rest in You.

He bids you return to Him,
to that place within,
where peace abides,
peace that is never disturbed;
to that place from which
Love never departs,
unless you depart from it.
Make your home in that place.

Late have I loved You,
Beauty ever old yet ever new!
Late have I loved You!
You were within me, but I was outside.
There I sought You, as I rushed about
among the beautiful things You had made.
You were with me,
but I was not with You.
The beautiful things of this world
kept me far from You.
You called. You cried.
You burst through my deafness.
You scattered my blindness.

I breathed Your fragrance
and now I pine for You.
I tasted You,
and I hunger and thirst for You.
You touched me,
and I burn with desire
for Your peace.

## Further reading

*The Confessions of St Augustine* translated by Maria Boulding OSB, Hodder & Stoughton, 1998

*St Augustine* by Garry Wills, Weidenfeld & Nicolson, 1999

*Christians in the World* by TJ van Bavel OSA Catholic Book Publishing Co., 1980

*Give What You Command* Michele Cardinal Pellegrino Catholic Book Publishing Co. (Now titled Spiritual Journey - Augustinian Press 1996)

*Augustine of Hippo*, by Mary T Clark - Geoffrey Chapman 2005

*Augustine, Major Writings*, Benedict J. Groeschel – Crossroads 1995